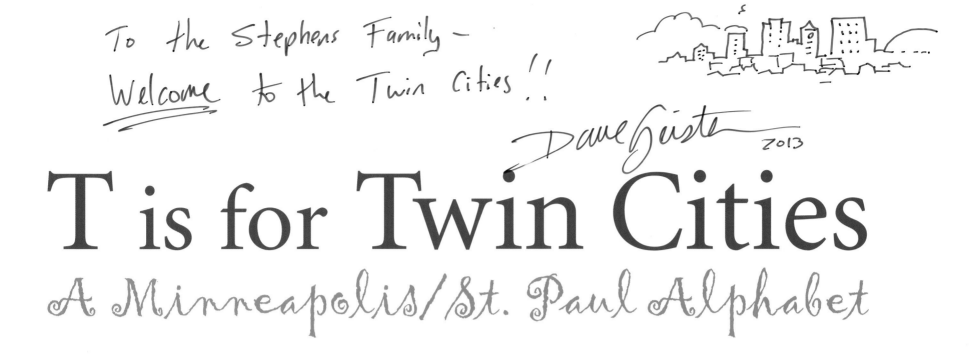

T is for Twin Cities
A Minneapolis/St. Paul Alphabet

Written by Nancy Carlson and Helen L. Wilbur
Illustrated by David Geister

ILLUSTRATOR'S ACKNOWLEDGMENTS

I could not have painted these illustrations without the family and friends who posed for me—Pat, Eva, Andy, Allie, Kevin, Zoe the Wiener Dog, Mike, A.J., and the whole Kisch family. Thanks also to Aaron Novodvorsky for his sound advice, my friends at Wet Paint, and my dear wife Pat who kept the world spinning on its axis while I hid in the studio.

DAVID

Text Copyright © 2012 Nancy Carlson and Helen L. Wilbur
Illustration Copyright © 2012 David Geister

Sleeping Bear Press®

315 E. Eisenhower Parkway, Suite 200
Ann Arbor MI 48108
www.sleepingbearpress.com

Sleeping Bear Press is an imprint of Gale, a part of Cengage Learning.

Printed and bound in the United States.

10 9 8 7 6 5 4 3 2 1

Library of Congress Cataloging-in-Publication Data

Carlson, Nancy L.
T is for Twin Cities: a Minneapolis/St. Paul alphabet / written by Nancy Carlson and Helen L. Wilbur; illustrated by David Geister.
p. cm.
ISBN 978-1-58536-583-8
1. Minneapolis Metropolitan Area (Minn.)—Juvenile literature. 2. Saint Paul Metropolitan Area (Minn.)—Juvenile literature. 3. Alphabet books. I. Wilbur, Helen L., 1948- II. Geister, David, ill. III. Title.
F614.M6C37 2012
977.6'579—dc23   2012007622

A is for Art

Here's a sight
to make you stop—
a spoonbridge fountain
with a cherry on top!

Wait, there's a 52-foot-long spoon with a thousand-pound cherry balanced on it. Are you at a giant's picnic? No, you are in the Minneapolis Sculpture Garden at the Walker Art Center. The spoon handle arches over a small pond and water sprays from the cherry. Installed in 1988, this dynamic sculpture by Claes Oldenburg and Coosje van Bruggen, called *Spoonbridge and Cherry*, has charmed and inspired residents and visitors wandering among and enjoying the many other sculptures in this open-air museum.

If you are an art lover, the Twin Cities is the place for you. You can stroll through galleries and museums to see classic work and contemporary pieces in a variety of media: drawing, painting, textiles, pottery, weaving, beads, and more. Have fun and enjoy beautiful things with a visit to such unique places as the Museum of Russian Art, the Gallery of Wood Art, and the Weisman Art Museum (with its curved metal exterior) located on the Mississippi River.

B is for Basilica

On a full city block,
majestic and grand
sits the first basilica
in our native land.

The Basilica of Saint Mary fills a city block in downtown Minneapolis with the beauty of its Beaux-Arts architecture, stained-glass windows, and huge copper dome. The architectural style, named for École des Beaux-Arts in Paris, is known for grand classical buildings with lavish ornamentation. Built between 1907 and 1915, it was the first basilica for the Catholic faith in the United States. Every year the basilica hosts a block party to promote volunteerism and community outreach programs. St. Paul has the Cathedral of Saint Paul, another excellent example of the Beaux-Arts style.

The Twin Cities are home to people of many faiths. Scandinavian immigrants brought their Christian religion, most notably Lutheran. More recent immigrants have brought Buddhism, Hinduism, and Islam to the Twin Cities. All have built their own unique houses of worship.

Bb

Good grief! You've likely heard of Charlie Brown, Lucy, Linus, the Great Pumpkin, and Snoopy. For nearly 50 years, cartoonist Charles M. Schulz wrote and drew the comic strip *Peanuts* for millions of fans all over the world.

Schulz, a native of the Twin Cities, started the comic strip as *Li'l Folks* in 1947 for a St. Paul newspaper. It was not an immediate success, but by Schulz's death in 2000, *Peanuts* had become one of the most beloved and enduring comics of all time. The *Peanuts* characters have appeared in more than 17,000 daily and Sunday newspaper comics, numerous television specials, a Broadway musical, greeting cards, books, and as all kinds of toys.

Charlie Brown's lack of confidence, Lucy's crabbiness, Pig Pen's dirt, and Snoopy's rich imagination are all part of our national culture. Schulz's characters live on in fans' hearts and in the bronze statues in St. Paul's Landmark Plaza.

Cc

C is for Charles Schulz

In Landmark Plaza
St. Paul downtown,
see Snoopy, Lucy,
and Charlie Brown.

Dd

D is for Dome

The golden horses,
and soaring dome
take you back to the majestic
monuments in Rome.

Minnesotans are justifiably proud of their grand capitol building on a bluff overlooking St. Paul. Opened in 1905, the architect Cass Gilbert modeled it after St. Peter's Basilica in the Vatican in Rome. The massive unsupported dome is made of marble. A gleaming statuary of gold leaf, steel, and copper, known as the quadriga, sits over the entrance. Quad means four and the quadriga has four huge horses pulling a chariot with human figures representing progress and prosperity.

Starting as a settlement with the humble name of Pig's Eye, St. Paul was selected as the capital when Minnesota became a state in 1858. Its location at the bend of the Mississippi River made it an important point for trade and transportation.

Although Minneapolis and St. Paul are known together as the Twin Cities, each has its own character.

E is for Exercise

We love to be outside
to skate and swim and run.
Our cities' parks and lakes
make fitness really fun.

Minneapolis and St. Paul residents are outdoor enthusiasts—year-round! After the long Minnesota winter, everyone can't wait to get outside. What better place to go than one of the 300 city parks? Public beaches and pools give residents of all ages a chance to swim and cool off in the summer heat. Golfers have a variety of beautifully maintained public courses to choose from. Both cities have active parks and recreation departments offering summer camps, programs, and opportunities to join a league to participate in your favorite sport.

Skating is popular in all seasons. Scott and Brennan Olson created the modern in-line roller skate in 1980. After perfecting their design, they began manufacturing the skates in their parents' basement, starting the Rollerblade™ Company and the in-line skating boom.

Whether you want to train for a marathon or just walk your dog, you can keep fit and experience the beauty of nature in the Twin Cities' parks.

F is for Foshay Tower

Foshay Tower's
art deco design
remains a landmark
on the city skyline.

Wilbur B. Foshay had a dream. He had built a fortune in public utilities, and he wanted to construct a skyscraper designed after the Washington Monument. When completed in August 1929, Foshay Tower was the tallest building in Minneapolis. Foshay hosted a three-day opening ceremony with lavish banquets, famous guests, and a military band to perform a march specially written by American composer John Philip Sousa. Foshay's triumph lasted only six weeks. His company failed in the financial turmoil during the Wall Street Crash of 1929.

Foshay's Tower dominated Minneapolis as its tallest building for nearly 50 years. Its distinctive obelisk shape of a four-sided tower with a pyramid on top and splendid art deco design made it a familiar sight on the cityscape. It is now a luxury hotel with an observation deck and museum open to the public.

Ff

Gg

The Guthrie Theater
wins the hearts
of those who love
dramatic arts.

After Sir Tyrone Guthrie, renowned British director, helped establish the Shakespeare Festival Theatre in Stratford, Ontario, he turned to the United States for a similar success. In 1959 he placed a small article in the drama section of the *New York Times* inviting cities across the United States to express interest in creating a major regional theater away from the commercialism of Broadway. The enthusiasm of the response from Minneapolis made the site selection easy.

The Guthrie Theater is dedicated to exploration of contemporary drama and new performance methods as well as to dynamic productions of classic plays. Many well-known actors got early professional training at the Guthrie, which also features an extensive theatrical education program.

Guthrie's innovative vision of open staging, based on Shakespeare's original productions, and a strong resident acting ensemble, has inspired similar projects throughout the US. The Guthrie Theater continues to perform to critical acclaim. In 2006 the theatre moved to a spacious new facility on the banks of the Mississippi River.

Nearly extinct a century ago, wild turkeys now thrive in urban and suburban areas of the Twin Cities. Flocks of these big birds have even been known to meander into Minnesota roadways and stop traffic. Hiking the city parks you may encounter them along with fox, deer, raccoons, muskrats, and hundreds of varieties of plants and birds.

Within minutes you can get away from the busy city streets and connect with nature. City and state parks have miles of trails that roam through the area's diverse ecosystems. Visit centers like the Minnesota Valley National Wildlife Refuge or the Eloise Butler Wildflower Garden and Bird Sanctuary to learn about the wilder residents of the Twin Cities.

At the Wildlife Rehabilitation Center of Minnesota, veterinarians and volunteers help injured and orphaned wild animals. You can follow the stories of the wild patients on the center's blog and visit during the annual open house.

H h

H is for Hiking

Hike the parks
and in the fall
you just might hear
a turkey call.

I i

I is for Ice

> Hurry, get your skates—
> laces tightly tied,
>   let's glide along the ice
> skating side by side.

Residents of the Twin Cities never let a little snow and ice keep them from enjoying the outdoors. From November to March and often into April, snow coats the land and the lakes freeze. There's always plenty to do. Cold-weather pastimes include tobogganing, ice boating, ice fishing, and snowshoeing. Of course, there's always skating and hockey. Youngsters often start to ice skate and play hockey as early as three or four years old.

St. Paul's Winter Carnival offers "The Coolest Celebration on Earth," featuring parades, ice sculptures, a dog sled rally, a giant snow slide, and even a treasure hunt. In Minneapolis the annual Lake Harriet Kite Festival in January gives kite enthusiasts an opportunity to show off their fabulous kites and demonstrate their kite-flying skills on the ice.

J j

Railroad executive James J. Hill became known as The Empire Builder for his expansion of the Great Northern Railway, which played a key role in the development of the American Northwest. He started as a clerk for a steamboat company and rose to be one of the most influential and wealthy businessmen of his day. In 1891 he built a lavish mansion on a bluff overlooking St. Paul, where he lived with his wife and ten children. Its 42 rooms feature exquisite carved oak and mahogany, stained-glass windows, and an art gallery complete with a pipe organ. Today it serves as a site for the Minnesota Historical Society.

Mr. Hill believed in the value of knowledge, hard work, and philanthropy. He founded and donated the James J. Hill Reference Library to the city of St. Paul. He wanted to pass along the keys to success to others with a library dedicated to practical business information. The library welcomes the public to use its resources free of charge.

J is for James J. Hill House

The Empire Builder's
        railroad expansion
    built a library
        and a splendid mansion.

Where in Minnesota can you shop at Bertha's Kitty Boutique and Ralph's Pretty Good Grocery, get your hair done at Curl Up and Dye, lunch at the Chatterbox Café, and pay your respects at the Statue of the Unknown Norwegian? Lake Woebegone, of course. But to take this trip you have to tune in the radio to *A Prairie Home Companion* on Saturday night and hear host Garrison Keillor give the latest news from this fictional small Minnesota town.

Since 1974 Keillor, guest musicians, and his ensemble cast have broadcast *A Prairie Home Companion* before a live audience. The show's home is the Fitzgerald Theater in St. Paul, but it travels to perform in auditoriums all over the country. Audiences enjoy familiar sketches like "Lives of the Cowboys" and "Guy Noir, Private Eye" interspersed with musical numbers and spoof commercials and accompanied by legendary live sound effects.

Garrison Keillor—poet, writer, and humorist— is known by his signature folksy speech, red shoes, and powerful storytelling. Every week he takes listeners to Lake Woebegon "where all the women are strong, all the men are good-looking, and all the children are above average."

K

k

K is for Keillor

He wears red shoes;
    he sings and writes
for his radio show
    on Saturday nights.

L is for Lakes

The sky and water
   sparkling blue.
Let's swim and
   paddle our canoe.

Minneapolis is known as the "City of Lakes." Lake Harriet, Lake Calhoun, Lake of the Isles, and Cedar Lake form the Chain of Lakes running through the heart of residential Minneapolis. The lakeshore is public property which makes it popular for many recreational activities like picnicking, swimming, fishing, boating, and canoeing. Public spaces also include beaches, park shelters, recreational facilities, historic markers, and miles and miles of trails.

The Grand Rounds Scenic Byway, a system of trails, paths, and roadways, loops for over 50 miles around the city of Minneapolis. The Chain of Lakes is one of the seven districts in one of the country's longest urban parkway systems. The trail follows the lake shores for walking, biking, and skating.

Each lake has its own character and offers unique scenery and activities. At Lake Harriet's Lyndale Park Gardens you can enjoy the formal rose garden and the peace garden In April and May you can observe the migratory birds that stop over at the Thomas Sadler Roberts Bird Sanctuary.

Ll

L

M is for Minnehaha Falls

Minnehaha, laughing waters,
named by the Dakota.
Come enjoy this great state park
when you visit Minnesota.

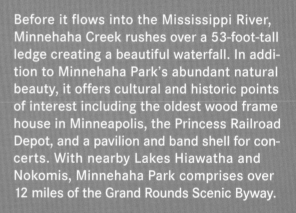

Before it flows into the Mississippi River, Minnehaha Creek rushes over a 53-foot-tall ledge creating a beautiful waterfall. In addition to Minnehaha Park's abundant natural beauty, it offers cultural and historic points of interest including the oldest wood frame house in Minneapolis, the Princess Railroad Depot, and a pavilion and band shell for concerts. With nearby Lakes Hiawatha and Nokomis, Minnehaha Park comprises over 12 miles of the Grand Rounds Scenic Byway.

In his narrative poem "The Song of Hiawatha," Henry Wadsworth Longfellow immortalized the names of the brave warrior Hiawatha, his love the maiden Minnehaha, and Hiawatha's mother Winona. The poem, written in 1855, presents an idealized vision of Native American life combining myths and legends from several tribes.

Generations before European contact, the Dakota Sioux culture flourished in the river valley. Their rich heritage continues today on tribal lands and communities. A sculptured mask of Chief Little Crow located in Minnehaha Park commemorates the chief who was killed following the Dakota Conflict.

N n

You can walk, shop, dine, catch a bus, check out a book at the library, or just sit and people watch on the Nicollet Mall in downtown Minneapolis. The only thing you can't do is drive a car on it! Summer brings the Minneapolis Farmer's Market on Thursdays where you can buy the best of local produce, honey, and fresh flowers. Celebrate the holiday season at the Holidazzle Parade. From Thanksgiving to Christmas, lighted floats, marching bands, choirs, and colorful characters light up the mall in a magical display.

Nicollet Avenue was named for Joseph Nicollet, a French geographer and cartographer who mapped the upper Mississippi River in the early 1800s. A large island in the Mississippi, Nicollet Island, was also named for him. This scenic spot right off Main Street in Minneapolis offers a lovely park, pavilion, romantic inn, and many historic homes.

N is for Nicollet Mall

Get a cup of hot chocolate
See the festive sights.
It's the Holidazzle parade—
marching bands and glittering ligh

Young residents of the Twin Cities learn about and make music with the Minnesota Orchestra. For more than 100 years, the Minnesota Orchestra Young People's Concerts have captivated and inspired students, schools, and families with favorites like *Hansel and Gretel* and *Peter and the Wolf.* Programs, in person and online, introduce young listeners to symphonic music and encourage young performers. Interactive *Kinder Konzerts* bring the joy of music to the littlest music lovers who are four and five years old.

Founded in 1903, the orchestra plays almost 200 performances each year on tour, broadcast on radio, or in its home hall in downtown Minneapolis. Over the years distinguished conductors have led this 98-musician ensemble in concerts and on recordings to critical acclaim. Summertime brings *Sommerfest,* offering a month of concerts with free performances of jazz, folk, and other musical genres outdoors on the plaza.

O is for Orchestra

The orchestra tunes from the lead violin. Listen, the concert's about to begin.

O o

Biscuits, bread, cookies, pie pastry—you can make them all with Pillsbury™ products. Charles Pillsbury started what was to become one of the most recognized food brands in the world in 1869 by purchasing a flour mill in Minneapolis. Combining the vast supply of grain in the Midwest with the power and transportation offered by the Mississippi River, Pillsbury quickly grew powerful and profitable. At one time Pillsbury claimed to have the largest flour mill in the world.

Now a part of General Mills™, Pillsbury runs a baking contest giving prizes to the best recipes in many categories. Two of Pillsbury's advertising icons—the Pillsbury Doughboy™ and the Jolly Green Giant™—are familiar to consumers everywhere.

The Twin Cities have a thriving business community of small- and medium-sized companies as well as large multinational corporations like Cargill™ and Target™.

P p

P is for Pillsbury

Let's go to the kitchen.
What is Grandma making?
Fresh from the oven,
the smell of biscuits baking.

Q q

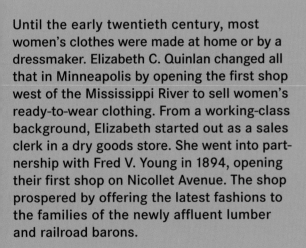

Q is for Quinlan

A smart businesswoman
with great fashion flair,
she had the first shop
selling ready-to-wear.

Until the early twentieth century, most women's clothes were made at home or by a dressmaker. Elizabeth C. Quinlan changed all that in Minneapolis by opening the first shop west of the Mississippi River to sell women's ready-to-wear clothing. From a working-class background, Elizabeth started out as a sales clerk in a dry goods store. She went into partnership with Fred V. Young in 1894, opening their first shop on Nicollet Avenue. The shop prospered by offering the latest fashions to the families of the newly affluent lumber and railroad barons.

Quinlan was elegant, tough, and demanding. She hired a top architect to design a new building for her store in 1926. The Young-Quinlan Department Store had chandeliers, marble staircases, and innovative underground parking and elevators to take customers directly to the selling floors. Quinlan called the building a "perfect gem" and it remains so today on Nicollet Mall. In a time when few women held positions of power, Quinlan became a dominant force in commerce and a strong supporter of charity and community service.

R r

Great cities grow near great rivers. The Twin Cities sit 13 miles apart on the banks of the Mississippi River. St. Paul developed at the northernmost point possible for ships to navigate on the river. Minneapolis started near the only falls on the Mississippi, using them to power mills for lumber and flour production.

From its headwaters in upper Minnesota, the Mississippi River flows south 2,320 miles and touches 10 states by the time it reaches the Gulf of Mexico. Used for commerce, transportation, water supply, and pleasure, the great river requires constant environmental, navigation, and flood management. A series of locks and dams between the Twin Cities make the river easier for boat traffic and shipping.

You can hike, bike, drive, or take your boat along the river to enjoy its majesty and beauty. Or you can go to the Guthrie Theater. The building features the Endless Bridge cantilevered over the landscape giving a breathtaking view of the river spilling over St. Anthony Falls.

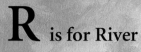

R is for River

From the cool north woods
  to the warm gulf shore,
the great river flows
  two thousand miles and more.

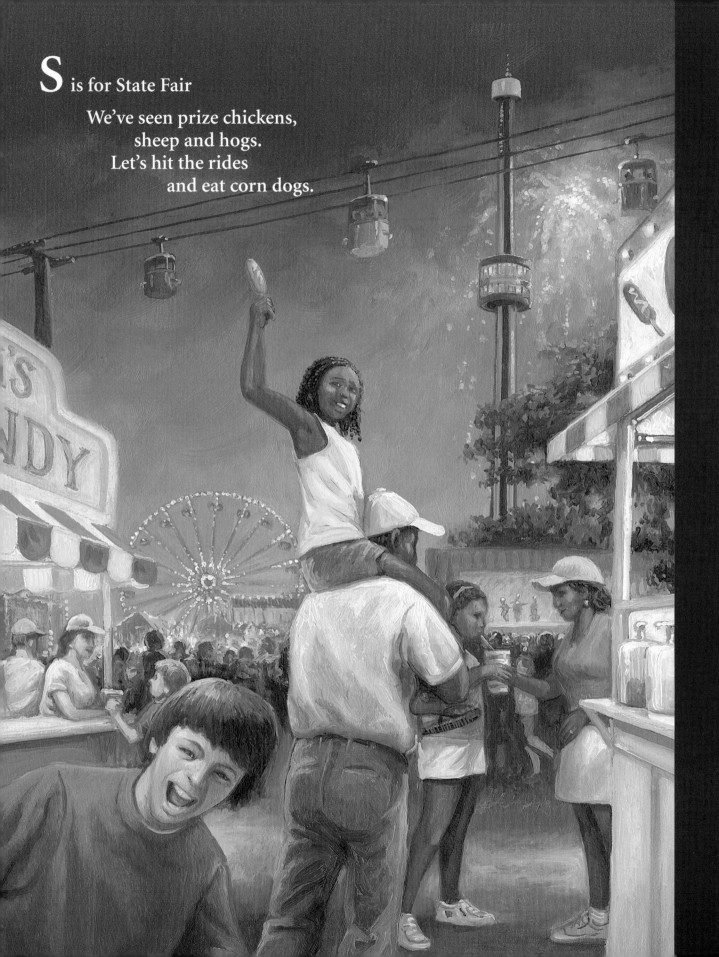

S is for State Fair

We've seen prize chickens,
sheep and hogs.
Let's hit the rides
and eat corn dogs.

For 12 days in late summer a crowd of more than 1.7 million people flocks to the Minnesota State Fair for the exhibits, fun, and food. The fair's traditions go back to the 1850s when Minnesota was still a territory. In 1885 the fair found a permanent home on a 320-acre site located halfway between the Twin Cities. The fair is still true to its original purpose of promoting farming, with livestock and agricultural produce competitions, machinery exhibitions, and a lot of 4-H activities. But there's much more to enjoy—concerts, talent shows, exciting rides, and, of course, food. Fairgoers can sample Minnesota culinary favorites as well as carnival food—a lot of which is deep fried and stuck on a stick.

One of the fair's most popular attractions takes place in a refrigerated rotating glass booth—butter sculpting. Twelve young women who work or live on Minnesota dairy farms compete to be the annual Princess Kay of the Milky Way. Each day of the fair, butter sculptor Linda Christensen carves a 90-pound block of butter into the likeness of one of the princesses.

S s

T is for Turnblad House

Turnblad's castle
   built with a mission—
a home, then a center
      for Swedish tradition.

T t

In the late 1900s poor harvests in Sweden caused a famine. The promise of low cost farmland in the American Midwest brought thousands of Swedish immigrants to Minnesota. One of them was eight-year-old Swan Turnblad who came with his family in 1868. Turnblad started work as a type-setter in Minneapolis for a Swedish language newspaper. He rose to become publisher, then sole owner of the *Svenska Amerikanska Posten,* making him a very wealthy man.

In 1908 Turnblad completed construction on a 33-room mansion that became known as the Turnblad Castle. The mansion features a carved mahogany interior and stained-glass windows. Large Swedish ceramic tile stoves heated many of the rooms. Turnblad also loved the latest technology and had central heating installed.

After living in the house for 21 years, Turnblad founded the American Swedish Institute and donated his mansion as its headquarters. The organization's mission is to preserve the history of the Swedish experience in America, share Swedish culture and traditions, and connect the community with modern Sweden.

The University of Minnesota, Twin Cities, founded in 1851, is a leading public research university. With more than 50,000 students and a wide range of academic offerings, the university draws faculty and students from around the world. The busy main campus is in Minneapolis on the east bank of the Mississippi River. The smaller West Bank campus focuses on business, law, and the arts. The campus in St. Paul is home to the College of Design and the veterinary school. The university offers a vibrant student experience with diverse activities and communities. Athletics for both men and women is a big part of student life at the University of Minnesota. The university's teams are known as the Golden Gophers.

With dozens of public and private institutions scattered across both towns, students have many choices for higher education in the Twin Cities. For example, Metropolitan State University and St. Paul College are public institutions. Two of many private universities are the University of St. Thomas and Hamline University.

U u

U is for University

Students from
across the nation
come for a first-rate
education.

V

V is for Vikings

Our champions the Vikings—
fearless like their name.
Fall Sundays you will find us
cheering every game.

Fans in the Twin Cities support their sports. Named for the fierce warriors from Scandinavia, the Minnesota Vikings first took the field in 1961 as part of the National Football League expansion. The Vikings' consistent winning record and the devotion of their fans make for exciting football. Over the years many great football legends have been part of the Vikings legacy—quarterback Fran Tarkenton, coach Bud Grant, and the defensive unit known as the "Purple People Eaters" referring to the team colors and their on-field toughness.

Summertime means baseball with the Minnesota Twins. Professional baseball got its start in the Twin Cities with minor-league teams in the late 1800s. In 1961 fans were delighted to welcome the relocation of the Washington Senators as the Minnesota Twins with Hall-of-Fame power-hitter Harmon Killebrew. Women made baseball history in Minneapolis in the 1940s with the All-American Girls Professional Baseball Leagues team the Millerettes, immortalized in the 1992 movie *A League of Their Own*.

Basketball fans can follow the NBA Timberwolves and the WNBA Minnesota Lynx.

Millions and billions and trillions of cats...

Millions of Cats, author and illustrator Wanda Gag's tale of an old couple searching for a cat companion, has enchanted millions of readers since its publication in 1928. After her father died when Wanda was 15, she used her writing and artistic skills to support her six brothers and sisters. Gag transformed the traditional children's book format which had text on one page and the picture on the other. She stretched the illustrations across two pages to propel readers through the story, making *Millions of Cats* an instant favorite, award winner, and beloved classic.

The Twin Cities have a strong publishing and reading community with a rich literary history. Famed authors F. Scott Fitzgerald and Anne Tyler were born in the area, while other beloved writers, like Kate DiCamillo, have adopted the cities as their home. Minneapolis is home to the Minnesota Center for the Book Arts as well as the Hennepin County Library System. The Friends of the St. Paul Public Library host the annual Minnesota Book Awards.

W is for Wanda Gag

She worked and drew
and wrote and that's
how she made her fame—
from millions of cats.

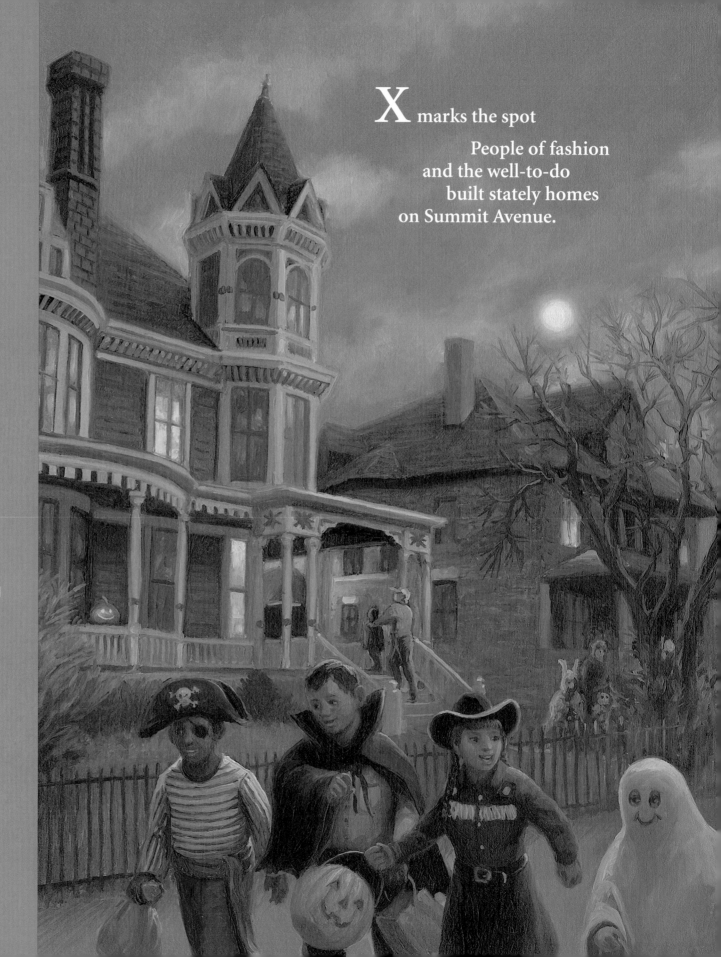

X x

X marks the spot

People of fashion
and the well-to-do
built stately homes
on Summit Avenue.

Stroll or drive down Summit Avenue in St. Paul for a trip to another era. This tree-lined street runs nearly five miles from downtown through the neighborhood where St. Paul's elite built their mansions. The expansion of the railroads and commerce in the late 1880s brought new wealth to many in a period called The Gilded Age. Wealthy families constructed stately homes along Summit Avenue to display their fortunes and position.

The Minnesota Governor's Mansion sits at 1006 Summit Avenue, an English Tudor of brick and stone, built in 1912 for lumberman and lawyer Horace Hills Irvine. His daughters donated it to the state in 1965 to serve as a residence for the sitting Minnesota governor.

Three houses on St. Paul's Summit Avenue are listed as National Historic Landmarks. One of them is the F. Scott Fitzgerald House. While the famous roaring twenties author of *The Great Gatsby* lived in several places in St. Paul, he lived here while writing his first novel, *This Side of Paradise*.

Yy

Whether you are visiting or living in the Twin Cities, you can find lots of things to do. From arts and culture to sports and outdoor activities, the Cities offer interesting activities all year-round.

Residents of the Twin Cities have a reputation for a reserved but friendly attitude that welcomes newcomers and builds strong communities. The earliest people to live in the area were native mound builders. Later the Dakota Sioux and Ojibwe nations settled the region on the banks of the Mississippi River. French Canadian fur traders and explorers were among the first Europeans to appear in the area, followed by migrations from England, Ireland, Scotland, Germany, and a large influx of immigrants from Scandinavia in the 1800s. More recently residents have emigrated from Africa and Southeast Asia.

If you live in the Twin Cities, you may trace your family back to the earliest inhabitants or be part of a vibrant new group of residents. Wherever your origins, you are part of a great city and community with diverse neighbors and lots of opportunities to grow, learn, and have fun.

Y is for You having fun

There's plenty of snow.
Let's slide down the hill.
I'll beat you to the bottom.
Oh boy, what a thrill!

Z is for Zero degrees

It's cold outside
but we don't care,
in warm boots and hats
and long underwear!

Because of their location in the northern central part of the continental United States, the Twin Cities experience colder winter weather than any large U.S. city, and that includes Anchorage, Alaska. The average winter temperature is 10 degrees Fahrenheit. The Cities also get a high degree of precipitation, which means winter blizzards sweeping down from the North Pole. Residents need to be handy with a snow shovel and wear layers of warm, waterproof clothing.

Summertime can bring extremes in the opposite direction with high heat and humidity. Summer evenings are often balmy and pleasant, bringing folks out to enjoy the long twilight after a day in the sun. But be prepared for the notorious mosquitoes.

Spring and fall provide lovely transitions from heat to cold. Bright, brisk fall days bring everyone out to see the leaves change with the message that winter is on its way. After the long winter, spring warmth thaws the roads and everyone's spirits.

Zz

Nancy Carlson

Nancy Carlson has spent her entire life in the Twin Cities area, and *T is for Twin Cities: A Minneapolis/St. Paul Alphabet* is her first book for Sleeping Bear Press. Nancy, the author and illustrator of more than 60 picture books, graduated from the Minneapolis College of Art and Design. She enjoys spending her spare time participating in outdoor activities around the beautiful lakes and parks that make the Twin Cities so enjoyable.

Helen L. Wilbur

A former librarian, Helen Wilbur has run a catering business, acted, taught school, sold cookware, and, for most of her career, worked on the electronic side of the publishing world. Helen has a BA in English Language and Literature from the University of Chicago and a master's degree from Columbia University in Library Science. Helen's books include *M is for Meow: A Cat Alphabet*, a 2007 ASPCA® Henry Bergh Children's Honor Book for illustration; *Z is for Zeus: A Greek Mythology Alphabet*, a 2009 Mom's Choice selection; *E is for Eiffel Tower: A France Alphabet*; *F is for Friendship: A Quilt Alphabet*; and *Lily's Victory Garden*, a 2011 IRA Teachers' Choices Reading List selection. Helen lives in New York City.

David Geister

More than 20 years ago, illustrator David Geister moved from his hometown of Prescott, Wisconsin to St. Paul, Minnesota. "Museums, book sellers, and art supply stores drew me like a magnet," he says, "and I don't think I could be happier anywhere else on earth!" Since 2000, he has lived in south Minneapolis, and every one of his several Sleeping Bear Press titles has been painted upstairs in the home he shares with his wife, author Patricia Bauer.